Manners in the Library

by **Carrie Finn**   illustrated by **Chris Lensch**

PiCTURE WiNDOW BOOKS
Minneapolis, Minnesota

Special thanks to our advisers for their expertise:

Kay Augustine, Associate Director
Institute for Character Development at Drake University

Susan Kesselring, M.A., Literacy Educator
Rosemount–Apple Valley–Eagan (Minnesota) School District

Editor: Nick Healy
Designer: Tracy Davies
Page Production: Brandie Shoemaker
Art Director: Nathan Gassman
Associate Managing Editor: Christianne Jones
The illustrations in this book were created digitally.

Picture Window Books
A Capstone Imprint
151 Good Counsel Drive
P.O. Box 669
Mankato, MN 56002-0669
877-845-8392
www.capstonepub.com

Printed in the United States of America in North Mankato,
Minnesota. 032010 005713R

Library of Congress Cataloging-in-Publication Data
Finn, Carrie.
Manners in the library / by Carrie Finn ; illustrated by
Chris Lensch.
p. cm. − (Way to be!)
Includes bibliographical references and index.
ISBN-13: 978-1-4048-3152-0 (library binding)
ISBN-13: 978-1-4048-3557-3 (paperback)
1. Library etiquette−Juvenile literature. 2. Etiquette for
children and teenagers. I. Lensch, Chris, ill. II. Title.
Z716.43.F56 2007
395.5'3−dc22   2006027564

Good manners are an important part of any library visit. Lots of different people use the library in lots of different ways. By using good manners, you can show respect for everyone.

There are many ways you can use good manners in the library.

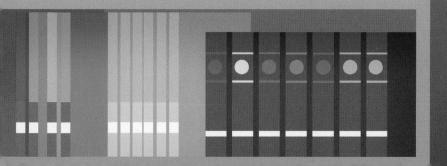

Mia uses her inside voice in the library. She keeps quiet so she won't disturb other people.

She is using good manners.

Charles wants to find a book on dinosaurs. He says "Please" when he asks a librarian for help.

He is using good manners.

Kyle is hungry, but he saves his apple until he leaves the library.

He is using good manners.

Ruth helps her little sister find a sing-along video. They are careful with the videos, books, and computers in the library.

They are using good manners.

Grace loves to learn about lions. Still, she checks out only the number of books she knows she'll read.

She is using good manners.

Jody spends a rainy day in the library. She reads silently to herself so she doesn't bother other people.

She is using good manners.

Mark's books are due on Friday.
He returns his books on time.

He is using good manners.

During story time, Joey and Tonya sit quietly and listen.

They are using good manners.

Manny does not interrupt his mom while she reads to his little brother.

He is using good manners.

You can learn a lot at the library. You can also have fun. By using good manners, you can make sure everyone else enjoys his or her visit, too.

Fun Facts

There are more than 117,000 libraries in the United States.

Mexico is home to the oldest library in North America.

The first known public library was in Egypt more than 2,000 years ago, in about 300 B.C.

The word "book" in Spanish is *libro*.

The word "library" in French is *bibliotheque*.

The Library of Congress has the most books of any library in the United States.

To Learn More

More Books to Read

DeGezelle, Terri. *Manners at the Library.* Mankato, Minn.: Capstone Press, 2005.

Elerding, Louise. *You've Got Manners!: Table Tips from A to Z for Kids of All Ages.* Burbank, Calif.: Grandy Publications, 2003.

Wheeler, Valerie. *Yes, Please! No, Thank You!* New York: Sterling, 2005.

On the Web

FactHound offers a safe, fun way to find Web sites related to topics in this book.

All of the sites on FactHound have been researched by our staff.

1. Visit *www.facthound.com*
2. Type in this special code: 1404831525
3. Click on the FETCH IT button.

Your trusty FactHound will fetch the best sites for you!

Index

asking for help, 7

caring for books, 10

checking out books, 13

eating in the library, 9

keeping quiet, 4, 14, 19

listening to stories, 19, 20

returning books, 16

using computers, 10

Look for all of the books in the Way to Be! series:

Being a Good Citizen: A Book About Citizenship

Being Fair: A Book About Fairness

Being Respectful: A Book About Respectfulness

Being Responsible: A Book About Responsibility

Being Trustworthy: A Book About Trustworthiness

Caring: A Book About Caring

Manners at School

Manners at the Table

Manners in Public

Manners in the Library

Manners on the Playground

Manners on the Telephone